CONTRIBUTORS TO THE BOOK

The National Galleries of Scotland extend
grateful thanks to the contractors who have
generously supported the publication of
this book, in particular the main sponsor,
Heery International Ltd.

Ace Elevators Ltd
ADT Fire & Security
Balfour Kilpatrick Ltd
Becker Geomatics Ltd
Curzon Interiors Ltd
Dane Architectural Systems Ltd
Edwards Engineering
The Gilmore Plastering Company
Heery International Ltd
Charles Henshaw & Sons Ltd
Thomas Johnstone Ltd
Keller Ground Engineering
Laing O'Rourke Scotland Ltd
Miller Roofing
Saxon Lifts Ltd
Watson Stonecraft
Wingate Electrical PLC

MICHAEL CLARKE

WITH PHOTOGRAPHY BY KEITH HUNTER

The Playfair Project

NATIONAL GALLERIES OF SCOTLAND

EDINBURGH · 2004

Foreword

The Playfair Project represents the most significant expansion of the Galleries' estates in recent years. This is not to forget the addition of the magnificent Dean Gallery in 1999, nor the establishment of partner galleries at Paxton House and Duff House in 1993 and 1995 respectively. Furthermore, our excellent new storage building, the Granton Centre, was opened in 2002. This project, however, is perhaps our most imaginative venture. By its very nature it takes us right back to the Galleries' beginnings, and represents a very satisfactory and potentially exciting conclusion to that story. The restoration of the Royal Scottish Academy Building and the creation of the underground Weston Link between it and the National Gallery provide us with a world-class exhibition space and superb visitor facilities in the very heart of Scotland's capital city. Thanks to the ingenious designs of John Miller a major new landmark has slipped discreetly into this World Heritage site.

Such an ambitious project is only made possible through the combined efforts and goodwill of many individuals and institutions. We are deeply grateful to the Scottish Office and its successor the Scottish Executive for their consistent support since the early 1990s. Successive Secretaries of State and First Ministers and their officials have been crucial to the project's success. Our neighbours in the Royal Scottish Academy have been most constructive, and particular thanks are due to their current President, Ian McKenzie Smith OBE. The Earl of Crawford and Balcarres nobly chaired a lengthy, but very productive, series of meetings between ourselves and the Academy. This took place during the period when Sir Angus Grossart CBE was our Chairman of Trustees and, thanks to this essential groundwork, his successor, the Rt Hon. the Countess of Airlie DCVO, was able to set the Playfair Project underway. The Heritage Lottery Fund and the Scottish Executive have both been major funders of the project. The remainder of the funds have come from many sources. A list of donors is provided in this book and we express our deepest gratitude to all of them for their magnificent public-spirited generosity. Nor would we overlook the many people who have given more modest amounts, for this reflects the wider public's support for, and interest in, the project. The sum raised represents the most successful fundraising campaign ever mounted by the National Galleries of Scotland. We would wish to acknowledge the hard work undertaken by Victoria Dickie, our first Director of Development, and continued by her successor Catrin Tilley. They have both worked closely with the Campaign Council kindly chaired by the Hon. Ranald Noel-Paton.

This project has represented a major effort by the Trustees and many of the staff of the National Galleries from across its wide range of departments. Above all it has been wholeheartedly led and overseen since its inception by its Director, Michael Clarke (also Director of the National Gallery of Scotland), ably assisted by the Project Adviser, Scott Robertson. Finally, we would like to thank those whose skills have brought the Playfair Project successfully to fruition, namely the architects John Miller and Su Rogers, and the many contractors who worked with our construction managers, Heery International Limited. A number of these firms have contributed to the production costs of this book and we are most grateful to them for their support.

When HRH Prince Albert laid the foundation stone of the National Gallery of Scotland in 1850, he set in train a sequence of events that would culminate in the re-opening of the restored Academy building in 2003 by HRH Prince Charles, Duke of Rothesay KG, KT (his great-great-great-grandson). This was followed in 2004 by the opening of the completed Playfair Project and Weston Link by HRH Prince Philip, Duke of Edinburgh KG, KT (his great-great-grandson on his mother's side). We thank their Royal Highnesses for their gracious participation in the history of these great buildings which are now set to play a pivotal role in the cultural history of Scotland.

SIR TIMOTHY CLIFFORD
Director-General, National Galleries of Scotland

BRIAN IVORY CBE
Chairman of the Trustees, National Galleries of Scotland

◀

The completed Playfair Project by night. The porticoes of William Henry Playfair's National Gallery of Scotland and Royal Scottish Academy Building are seen below Edinburgh Castle, with the new Weston Link below.

The Playfair Project

Consultants and Contractors

ARCHITECTS

John Miller and Partners, London
John Miller
Su Rogers
John Carpenter
Stuart Hill

The London-based partnership was formed in 1961, initially as Colquhoun and Miller, and on Alan Colquhoun's retirement in 1989 became John Miller and Partners. The practice has concentrated on public buildings and has become a specialist in the design of art galleries. It has previously designed improvements to three of London's most significant art spaces. The new twentieth-century galleries at the National Portrait Gallery were completed in 1993, the reorganised and upgraded Serpentine Gallery in Kensington Gardens opened to great public acclaim in 1998 and their substantial restoration and enlargement of Tate Britain was completed in 2002. Other notable projects have included the Stevens Building in the Royal College of Art, London, and the Scott Polar Research Institute, Cambridge University. A number of important arts and education based projects reached completion in the summer of 2004. Newnham College Library, Cambridge and the Fitzwilliam Museum Courtyard Development, Cambridge were opened in June and July respectively, and the Playfair Project, Edinburgh was completed in August.

CONSERVATION ARCHITECTS

Simpson and Brown, Edinburgh
James Simpson
Lesley Kerr

CONSTRUCTION MANAGERS

Heery International Ltd
Robbie Smith
Ken Hamilton
Michael McSorley
Jim McWilliams
David Officer
Alex Omond
Mike Smith
Debbie Webster
Melanie Welsh

STRUCTURAL ENGINEERS

Anthony Hunt Associates, London
Les Postawa
Malachy Macnamara
David Weale

M&E ENGINEERS

SVM
David Liptrot
Craig Thomas

COST CONSULTANTS

Davis Langdon,
London and Edinburgh
Rob Smith
Neil Dickson
Samantha Dickson
Greig Jamieson
Erland Rendall
Jody Wilkinson

PROJECT MANAGERS

Bovis Lend Lease, Edinburgh
Malcolm Mathieson
Joseph McGlynn
David Prudence

LANDSCAPE ARCHITECTS

Derek Carter Associates, Edinburgh
Derek Carter

TRADE CONTRACTORS

Ace Elevators Ltd
ADT Fire & Security
Balfour Kilpatrick Ltd
Becker Geomatics Ltd
Bell Decorating
Curzon Interiors Ltd
Dane Architectural Systems Ltd
Draftseal Ltd
ECG Group
Edwards Engineering
Elliot Redispace
The Gilmore Plastering Company
Charles Henshaw & Sons Ltd
Invensys
Keller Ground Engineering
Kelsey Roofing
John Kennedy Engineering
Laing O'Rourke Scotland Ltd
Levolux AT Ltd
Lyndon Scaffolding PLC
McGrath Group
Miller Roofing
Mivan Ltd
O'Neill Cleaning Ltd
Premier One Landscaping
Saxon Lifts Ltd
James Scott and Sons (Kitchen Equipment) Ltd
Thomas Johnstone Ltd
Watson Stonecraft
Wingate Electrical PLC

The Playfair Project

Michael Clarke *Director, National Gallery of Scotland*

WILLIAM HENRY PLAYFAIR

In the heart of Edinburgh sit two elegant neo-classical temples devoted to the fine arts – the Royal Scottish Academy Building (formerly the Royal Institution) and the National Gallery of Scotland. Both were designed by William Henry Playfair (1790–1857), one of the greatest Scottish architects of the nineteenth century, whose distinctive and original designs helped to transform the appearance of nineteenth-century Edinburgh into that of a 'modern Athens'.

After winning the competition to complete Robert Adam's designs for Edinburgh University in 1817, Playfair collaborated with Charles Robert Cockerell on the creation of an exact facsimile of the Parthenon to crown Calton Hill in 1824. Sadly, never completed due to a lack of funds, this melancholic relic now surveys from its windswept heights many of Playfair's greatest achievements in Scotland's capital. To the south lies the startlingly original Surgeons' Hall (1830–2) and to the west the 'Jacobethan' Donaldson's Hospital (1842–54).

Playfair's abilities as an urban planner can be seen in the Calton Hill development and that of Royal Circus with the idiosyncratic profile of St Stephen's Church (1827–8) closing off the vista at the bottom of Howe Street.

Playfair was acutely conscious of the compositional consequences of his designs, which were sensitively fitted into the existing cityscape. Nowhere is this more evident than at the Mound site, situated at the very heart of Edinburgh, with which Playfair's name is irrevocably associated. Overlooking this area is his 'Gothic' Free Church College (1846), which reflects the pervading character of the late medieval Old Town immediately behind. Below, axially aligned, sit the National Gallery and the Royal Scottish Academy, their classicism linked perfectly with the Georgian New Town to the north. The histories of these two buildings are inextricably linked, but their full potential has only now been realised with the completion of the Playfair Project, nearly a century and a half after Playfair's death.

◄

Alexander Nasmyth
1758–1840
Princes Street with the Commencement of the Building of the Royal Institution, 1825 (detail)
National Gallery of Scotland, Edinburgh

The painting shows the architect William Henry Playfair, seen from behind, directing operations during the early stages of construction of the Royal Institution (later known as the Royal Scottish Academy).

►

Henry Winkles
(active 1819–1832)
This contemporary print shows the original block-like design of Playfair's Royal Institution building.

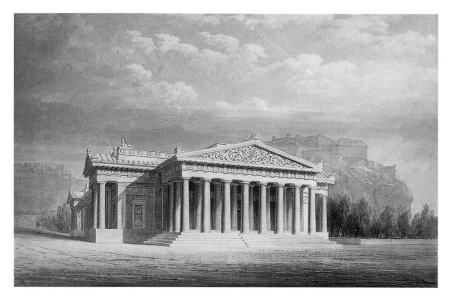

George Meikle Kemp
1795–1844
The Royal Institution (now the Royal Scottish Academy), Edinburgh, 1839
National Gallery of Scotland, Edinburgh

This drawing by the architect George Meikle Kemp shows Playfair's design of the northern elevation of the Royal Institution building. The sphinxes, designed by the sculptor Sir John Steell, were installed on the roof in 1837.

Steell's statue of Queen Victoria, one of the earliest public sculptures of the young queen, was installed some years later in 1844. This massive statue weighs twenty-five tons and cast iron beams had to be added to the portico to support it.

HISTORY

In the beginning there was neither a Gallery nor an Academy but an Institution. The Institution for the Encouragement of the Fine Arts in Scotland, founded in 1819, aimed to promote artistic enlightenment through loan exhibitions, consisting of works by the old masters borrowed from aristocratic collections. The popularity of these shows, held in a variety of temporary venues in Edinburgh, led to the decision to provide a permanent home in which to house them. Accordingly, in 1822 Playfair was commissioned by the Government's Board of Manufactures to design the Institution building on Princes Street, which opened to the public in early 1826. It was rather a block-like structure, the design of which suggests certain parallels with modern German architecture of the period. Its first occupants were the Institution, the Trustees' Academy (predecessor of the present Edinburgh College of Art), the Scottish Society of Antiquaries and the Royal Society of Edinburgh. Unsurprisingly, it rapidly required enlargement, which was duly carried out by Playfair in the early 1830s. He used

William Henry Playfair
1790–1857
A design for the National Gallery of Scotland
National Gallery of Scotland, Edinburgh

This drawing illustrates how Playfair's proposed new building would look against the rugged grandeur of Edinburgh Castle. Although the design for the National Gallery was based on ancient classical sources, the historical backdrop of the Castle Rock only served to highlight the modernity of Playfair's new building.

this opportunity to transform the style of the exterior giving it a much more classical feel with triangular pediments, porticoes and additional Doric columns.

Although the Institution committee had been buying some works from contemporary Scottish artists, many of the latter had formed their own Scottish Academy (granted its 'royal' charter in 1838). In 1835 the Academy was granted permission to lease some of the galleries in the Institution building. This solution rapidly proved inadequate, however. In addition, there developed an understandable conviction that Scotland, like England,

friend and associate David Ramsay Hay.

The physical distribution of the various bodies involved in this complex game of musical chairs was rather different from the configuration that can be found today. The National Gallery and the Royal Scottish Academy originally shared the Gallery building, the former occupying the western side and the latter the two main suites of octagonal rooms on the eastern side of the building . The Royal Institution housed a total of four other bodies. This arrangement continued until the early twentieth century when further change became necessary.

◄

Sir David Young Cameron
1865–1945
The National Gallery of Scotland and the Royal Scottish Academy, 1916
National Gallery of Scotland, Edinburgh

Playfair's two buildings on the Mound created a picturesque effect and enhanced the natural beauty of the site. Playfair believed that the buildings should not invade the landscape and that where possible they should blend into the scenery with the use of natural planting of trees and shrubs – an effect admirably achieved here in the heart of Edinburgh.

should have its own National Gallery.

The foundation stone of Playfair's new National Gallery of Scotland, lying just to the south of the Institution building, was laid by HRH Prince Albert on 30 August 1850. The building finally opened to the public on 22 March 1859. In contrast to the Institution building, Playfair's choice of classical order for the National Gallery was the Ionic, and the warmer honey-coloured sandstone came from Binny Quarry, West Lothian, as opposed to the cooler Craigleith stone used for the Institution. The Institution's collection of old master paintings was transferred to form part of the founding collection of the National Gallery; the interiors of which had been designed by Playfair's

Following the National Gallery of Scotland Act of 1906, which created a Board of Trustees of the Gallery, a Parliamentary Order of 1910 ('The Appropriation of Buildings') removed the Academicians from the Gallery building and gave them permanent tenancy of office space in the Institution building and the right to hold an annual exhibition there. The Institution was thereafter to be known as the 'Royal Scottish Academy', the management of which was vested with the Trustees of the National Gallery of Scotland. The bodies thereby displaced from the Institution were found alternative accommodation. This change-round necessitated further architectural modification of Playfair's two buildings: the

Gallery and what can, from that point on, accurately be called the Academy. This was carried out most successfully by, perhaps, the unsung hero of the architectural history of these two great buildings.

William Thomas Oldrieve (1853–1922) was, at the time, HM Principal Architect to the Scottish Ministry of Works. Amongst his achievements can be numbered the main post office buildings in Edinburgh and Glasgow. In his rearrangement of the National Gallery he created a central northern entrance (dispensing with the two previous entrances to the 'Gallery' and 'Academy' sides of the building) and installed a low, central, hexagonal entrance hall, the ceiling of which was pierced by an oculus through to new gallery space above, which was reached by a graceful swept staircase. In the Academy he was even more interventionist, creating a two-storey layout throughout in place of Playfair's idiosyncratic original spaces and thereby determining the internal layout of the building

▲

The stylish cover of the catalogue for the **Braque** *exhibition held at the Royal Scottish Academy during the Edinburgh International Festival of 1956.*

which, to a considerable degree, it retains to this day. In both the National Gallery oculus and the Academy's entrance hall stairs and balustrade he used dwarf Ionic columns to elegant effect. The upper-floor galleries in the Academy were interlinked by an ingenious series of diagonal and rectilinear openings which articulated the interior space and provided a fascinating variety of views through from one space to another. In the centres of these galleries were banquettes arranged around hot-air vents. Thus, when the Gallery and Academy were reopened to the public in 1912, the former was devoted to the nation's permanent collection of European and Scottish art, whereas the latter was essentially a temporary exhibition space used by the Royal Scottish Academy and a number of other exhibiting societies. At first glance it would appear that Scotland had devised the perfect, logical answer to its various needs in these respective spheres. However, this arrangement, it would transpire, had been laid on faulty foundations.

THE RISE OF EXHIBITIONS

It seems that from the beginning the relationship between the Gallery and Academy was administratively, if not physically, distant; each understandably went its own way. The Gallery concentrated on building up its already formidable permanent holdings, but it did not engage in the business of staging temporary exhibitions. Nor did it concern itself overmuch with the administration of the Academy building, where the Academicians were largely left to their own devices. In addition to the exhibitions mounted by the Academy, there was also an increasing number of shows staged by other societies, in particular the Society of Scottish Artists, which had been founded in 1891. Not only did the Society exhibit its own members' works but, in the earlier part of the twentieth century, it staged what were, for Edinburgh, ground-breaking exhibitions of *Munch* (1931) and *Klee* (1934) amongst others. The Society continued to show European artists of note up to the outbreak of the Second World War which, understandably, proved something of a watershed in the Academy's history.

A major new chapter opened in 1947 with the establishment, in a postwar spirit of optimism and renewal, of the Edinburgh International Festival. A close association between the Festival Society, the Royal Scottish Academy and the newly created Arts Council of Great Britain led to a spectacular series of summer exhibitions in the Academy building beginning, in 1952, with *Degas*. Among the successes which followed were shows on Dufy, Cézanne, Gauguin, Braque, and a Monet exhibition that attracted 50,000 visitors in four weeks in 1957. Not to be outdone, the Academy independently mounted shows of true significance, including one on the German Expressionist movement *Der Blaue Reiter*. And all this took place against a Festival background which embraced such musical luminaries as Bruno Walter, Kathleen Ferrier, Sir Thomas Beecham and Ferenc Fricsay, to name but a few.

By the mid-1960s, however, attendances at festival exhibitions had begun to drop away significantly, though the exhibitions put on by the various Scottish artists' societies continued unabated. The 1980s saw a major policy shift with the National Galleries asserting their desire to mount shows in the Academy building to coincide with the festival. The first of these were *Francis Picabia 1879–1953* and *The Magic Mirror: Dada and Surrealism from a Private Collection* (1988), and further shows of note included *Miró Sculptures* (1992) and *The Romantic Spirit*

in German Art 1790–1990 (1994). In addition, an important series of shows was devoted to Scottish Art: *William McTaggart 1835–1910* (1989), *Scotland's Pictures* (1990), *Virtue and Vision: Sculpture and Scotland 1540–1990* (1991), *The Line of Tradition* (1993) culminating in *Light from the Dark Room: A Celebration of Scottish Photography* (1995). This renewed exhibition activity was fatally compromised, however, by the continuing deterioration of the physical state of the building, which increasingly failed to measure up to internationally agreed criteria for exhibition venues.

CRACKS APPEAR

There was an underlying physical problem. Playfair had based his foundations for the Academy building on the 'Venetian raft' method, whereby a network of supporting wooden piles and a lattice mattress had been placed in the compacted earth (spoil from the New Town construction) that formed the causeway, known as the Mound, between the Old and New Towns. By the closing years of the twentieth century the majority of these wooden supports had gradually rotted, leaving a complex network of voids under the building and causing severe subsidence, particularly in the north-east corner where large cracks were visible in the interior plasterwork. Sadly, the problems did not stop there. The roof, which had been com-

▶
The exhibition Scotland's Pictures *organised by the National Galleries of Scotland and held at the Royal Scottish Academy in 1990 showing the galleries prior to restoration.*

pletely renewed in Oldrieve's 1910–12 campaign, leaked badly in several places – to the extent that buckets had to be positioned under the roof lights during particularly severe rainstorms. The glazing in the top-lighting was dangerously defective. There was no air-conditioning and portable humidifying units had to be temporarily installed. The building did not then meet current exhibiting standards and ceased to be used as an international venue.

REMEDIAL ACTION

The urgent need for remedial action regarding the state of the Royal Scottish Academy Building was first officially acknowledged in 1990 by the then Secretary of State for Scotland, Malcolm Rifkind. Shortly thereafter his successor, Ian Lang, set up, under the chairmanship of the Earl of Crawford and Balcarres, a joint committee of senior representatives from the National Gallery and the Royal Scottish Academy. They were charged with finding a workable solution to the restoration and proper use of the building. The committee met no less than thirteen times between 1993 and 1996, and eventually agreed on a proposal that involved renovating the upper galleries and creating a new suite of exhibiting rooms on the lower floors in spaces then being used for storage. The National Gallery, building on this agreement, was acutely conscious of the potential of the whole site for further development and commissioned an architectural and structural report from Keppie Architects. These plans were then worked up into a series of option appraisals for the Scottish Office (as it was then called) to consider. They consisted of the following:

1. Do nothing.

2. Repair the Academy building's foundations and make it wind and watertight.

3. Upgrade the Academy building to full international exhibiting standards.

4. Option three, with the addition of an underground link between the Academy and the National Gallery in which would be housed much-needed visitor facilities.

The Galleries' strong preference was for option

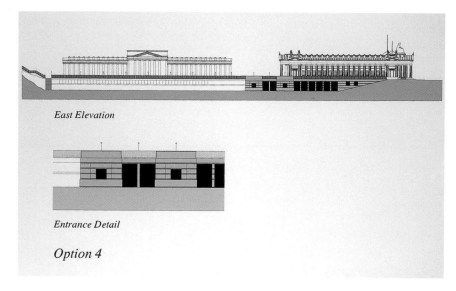

East Elevation

Entrance Detail

Option 4

four, as this had the potential to provide a full range of urgently needed visitor facilities in addition to the world-class exhibition spaces envisaged in the Academy building. During the period in which the Galleries' proposals were being considered there was a change of government in Westminster and a Scottish parliament was established, whose devolved responsibilities included the national arts bodies in Scotland. It was, therefore, the Scottish Minister for Education, Sam Galbraith, who announced in 1999 that government preference was for 'something between options two and three' and that £10,000,000 would be provided by the Scottish Executive to that end. This vouchsafed restoration of the Academy building to a satisfactory standard, but included no visitor facilities, most notably lacking in the field of education. The Galleries took it upon themselves to find the additional funding with which to develop a solution that took option four as its basis. A £7,000,000 application was made to the Heritage Lottery Fund and, after much hard work, this was successfully granted in 2000. The remaining monies necessary for the completion of the project would, it was decided, be found by the Galleries from private institutions and individuals. Although the Galleries had a well-deserved reputation for fundraising as far as the acquisition of works of art was concerned, the Playfair Project presented a formidable new challenge. A Campaign Council and a Committee of Honour were created and a detailed fundraising campaign was put in place.

▲

Option four from the structural and architectural report prepared by Keppie Architects. The plan shows an underground link connecting the National Gallery of Scotland and the Royal Scottish Academy Building. The possibility of such a link had already been established in the 1980s by means of geotechnical tests instructed by the Director of the National Galleries, Timothy Clifford.

The desire to restore the Academy building and provide first-class visitor services should be viewed within the context of the overall history of the National Galleries of Scotland. The National Gallery of Scotland first opened to the public in 1859 and by the mid-1990s, the Galleries had grown considerably. The collection continued to increase in number and variety and the estate expanded accordingly. The first addition was the Scottish National Portrait Gallery in Queen Street in 1889, the second was the Scottish National Gallery of Modern Art, which was established in 1960 and housed, initially, in Inverleith House in the Royal Botanic Garden, then permanently relocated in 1984 to the former John Watson's school in Belford Road. The Gallery of Modern Art acquired a sister institution, the Dean Gallery in 1999. Of all these Galleries, however, it was the National Gallery that had fallen furthest behind in terms of the services it could provide to the visiting public. It had limited toilet facilities, no restaurant or cafeteria and, perhaps worst of all, no education facilities.

The National Gallery had been partially enlarged in 1978 with the addition of the semi-underground 'New Wing', whose dual purpose was to display the outstanding pictures from the Scottish collection and also to provide an area for temporary exhibitions. Significantly, it was the second function which took precedence when the New Wing first opened to the public with an outstanding exhibition entitled *The Discovery of Scotland*. Although the space was reasonably well suited to the display of the permanent collection, it rapidly became apparent that, for more popular shows such as *Degas* (1979), *Lighting up the Landscape* (1986), *Cézanne and Poussin* (1990) and *From Monet to Matisse* (1994) it was woefully inadequate, being too small and having very cramped access. Furthermore, every time a temporary exhibition was mounted in the New Wing the Scottish paintings had to be taken down, to the dismay and disappointment of many visitors to the Gallery.

▼

The 'New Wing' extension to the National Gallery of Scotland, which was completed in 1978. The space had a dual purpose: to display the outstanding pictures from the Scottish collection, and to provide an area for temporary exhibitions.

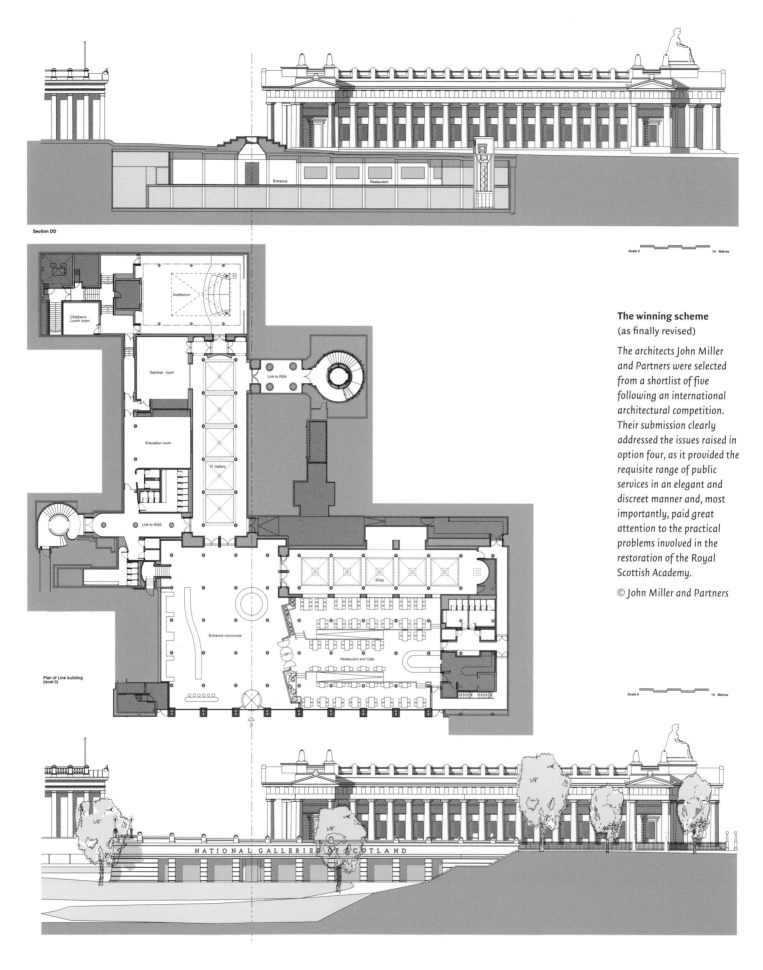

Section DD

Scale 0   10 Metres

Auditorium

Children's Lunch room

Seminar room

Education room

1st Gallery

Link to RSA

Link to NGS

Entrance concourse

Shop

Restaurant and Cafe

Plan of Link building
(level 0)

Scale 0   10 Metres

The winning scheme
(as finally revised)

The architects John Miller and Partners were selected from a shortlist of five following an international architectural competition. Their submission clearly addressed the issues raised in option four, as it provided the requisite range of public services in an elegant and discreet manner and, most importantly, paid great attention to the practical problems involved in the restoration of the Royal Scottish Academy.

© John Miller and Partners

NATIONAL GALLERIES OF SCOTLAND

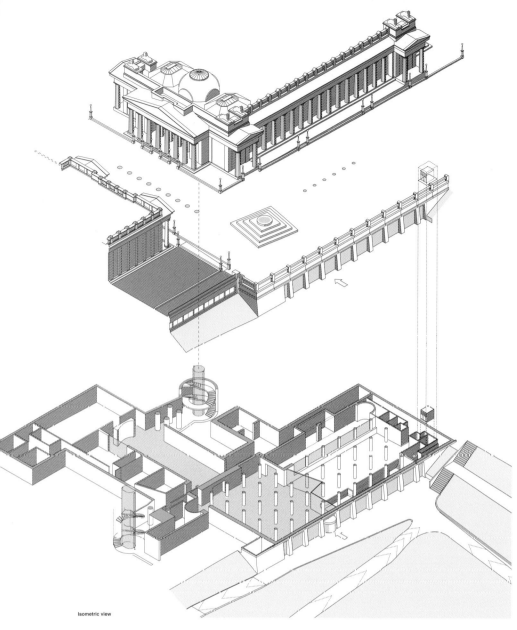

Isometric view

THE COMPETITION

Once the Trustees had taken the decision to proceed with option four and government approval had been secured, a project team was set up and a competition was held to appoint an architectural practice to design the project. It was decided that the project should be named after the architect of the buildings it would link, William Henry Playfair. From a long list of over fifty applicants, five finalists were selected and invited to submit detailed designs. The jury eventually selected the London-based practice of John Miller and Partners whose submission clearly addressed the issues raised in option four, provided the requisite range of public services in an elegant and discreet manner and, most importantly, paid great attention to the practical problems involved in the restoration of the Academy building. Noteworthy among the other finalists' proposals were the Dutch firm Meccanoo's sunken, stepped piazza between the two buildings; Simpson and Brown's (with Pawson Williams) weighty proposed entrance building from East Princes Street Gardens; Sir Terry Farrell's underground concourse beneath the precinct linking both sides of Princes Street Gardens; and finally Richard Murphy's (with Law and Dunbar-Nasmith) ambitious, cascading two-storey entrance into East Princes Street Gardens.

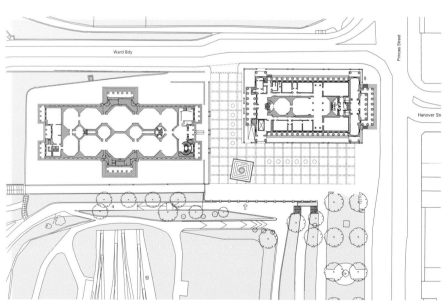

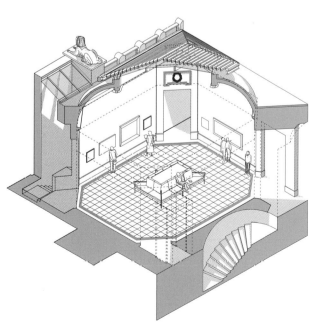

Computer simulation of the proposals for the Playfair Project, showing a cutaway view of the Weston Link and the refurbished galleries of the Royal Scottish Academy.

Before any work could commence on the main project, however, the foundations of the Academy building, seriously compromised by voids and subsidence, had to be secured. The firm of Keller Ground Engineering was engaged to inject concrete grout into the cavities beneath the building. This preliminary phase was begun in 1999 and involved digging a parallel trench to the east of the building from which a network of intersecting

pipes was bored underneath the Academy. These pipes had holes at regular intervals through which concrete grout was forced at high pressure into the voids beneath the building. This relatively new technique of soil fracture compensation grouting had been perfected by Keller's during the work they undertook on London Underground's Jubilee Line extension. By June 2000 a third of a million litres of grout had been injected in this manner and the Academy building was secure.

As far as the main building contract was concerned, it was eventually decided to use the Construction Management system and the firm of Heery International was duly appointed to undertake this on the Galleries' behalf. Heery's would therefore supervise all the specialist contractors engaged on the project and work in close collaboration with the client and the design team.

Work on the Academy building encompassed two main areas: the repair and restoration of the original historical fabric, and the alterations and installations required to make the building suitable for international exhibitions. For the most part these were carried out concurrently and at various stages there were almost forty different trade contractors on site.

Before any new work could be undertaken a considerable part of the original building, especially at the south end, had to be removed – in particular the roof, internal walls, intermediate floor, lower landings and foundations down to

◄

The work to underpin the foundations of the Royal Scottish Academy Building began in March 1999. The preliminary phase involved digging a trench on the east side of the building, from which a network of intersecting pipes was bored underneath the Academy. These pipes contained holes at regular intervals through which concrete grout was forced at high pressure filling the voids beneath the building.

►

Prior to any new work being undertaken a considerable part of the original Academy building had to be removed – in particular sections of the roof and internal walls.

◄ Preparation for the new lift shaft at the southern end of the Academy building.

► As the refurbishment of the Royal Scottish Academy reached completion, work started on phase two of the project. This shows the tower crane used in the excavation of the Link building.

◄ A view through to the aperture in the south-east corner of the Academy building, cut to accommodate the massive door of the art-handling lift.

► The complexity of the work required is shown by the large steel prop needed to support the south portico of the Royal Scottish Academy as the new stair and lift were dug out.

►► Building work in progress on the sadly dilapidated upper galleries in the Academy building. Internally, the upper spaces were little altered but benefited from new wall surfaces, versatile lighting systems and air-conditioning.

below the lowest link building level – in order to allow for the construction of a new circular stair and lift. This also necessitated the reconfiguration of various entrances and internal galleries. Concurrent with this was the preparation of the roof for the installation of insulation, new coverings, and roof lights which would be double glazed and UV filtered. They would also be provided with powered external louvres in order to control daylight and thereby afford protection to light-sensitive artworks. In the valleys between the gallery domes strengthening work was carried out to allow the installation of new services, including chillers and air handling units to control temperature, humidity and filtration, and a boiler-house underneath John Steell's statue of Queen Victoria.

Externally, repairs and restoration included the removal of vegetation, graffiti and some of the recent alterations and fixtures to the building. There was also careful conservation of much of the original stonework and repairs to pointing and carving. Loose stone was fixed, but there was relatively little indenting of new stones. In addition to that required on the stonework, considerable work was needed on the doors and windows. The cast iron railings and lamp standards, which had been removed in the early twentieth century, were reinstated to Playfair's original designs, thereby considerably improving the external appearance of the building, as well as discouraging the unwelcome activities of skateboarders and of vandals, who had hitherto disfigured the stonework with graffiti.

Internally, the most radical changes involved the creation of an elegant circular stair and lift at the south end, seen through a huge window in gallery two on the upper floor. Otherwise, the upper gallery spaces were little altered but benefited from new wall surfaces, versatile lighting systems, subtly introduced air-conditioning and, most visibly, new oak flooring and restored Edwardian mahogany dados. From a technical point of view, one of the most ingenious elements was the installation of a goods lift for handling artworks, accessed through a 'stone' door, cunningly concealed in the south-east portico. Within the lower floor, new galleries were created out of former storerooms and workshops, recreating something of Playfair's original scheme.

◄

View across the sculpture court to the refurbished galleries beyond.

►

One of the most radical changes involved the creation of an elegant circular stair and lift at the south end of the building, visible through a huge window in gallery two on the upper floor.

◄

View from the new staircase through the window into the gallery space beyond.

▶

View through the galleries showing the new oak flooring and the restored Edwardian dados. The original sightlines of Oldrieve's scheme were restored by removing the temporary screens, which had subsequently been installed in the corners of the galleries.

The first phase of the project, the refurbishment and upgrading of the Academy building, was successfully completed in August 2003. The opening exhibition *Monet: The Seine and The Sea*, sponsored by the Royal Bank of Scotland, occupied most of the upper galleries of the Academy and attracted record crowds of over 170,000 during its three month run. Over seventy paintings by Monet from collections all round the world were included, together with a number of works by significant predecessors and contemporaries. The exhibition examined a crucial period in Monet's career from 1878 to 1883 when he was largely based in the rural village of Vétheuil on the River Seine, just a few miles from Giverny. The show provided a crucial test of the new facilities in the building such as the new goods lift, air-conditioning, security and lighting, all of which performed to the desired standard. Both the exhibition and the project were featured in a television programme broadcast on Scottish Television in July 2003. Prior to the exhibition opening there was a grand donors' dinner on the evening of 4 August 2003. Earlier that day the building and exhibition had been officially opened by H R H the Prince of Wales, Duke of Rothesay. The new lower galleries were inaugurated with a display, drawn from the National Gallery of Scotland's holdings, on the history of the Gallery and Academy buildings.

For the duration of the building works to the Academy the Academicians had been temporarily accommodated in premises in Waterloo Place, Edinburgh. In the summer of 2003 they moved back into their office space in the main Academy building and also took possession of their library, which they had independently commissioned John Miller to renovate to a mutually agreed design.

*Views of the new lower galleries. The top photograph shows the exhibition **A Pleasing Prospect: A History of the Mound and its Buildings** with works drawn from the National Gallery of Scotland's holdings on the history of the Gallery and Academy buildings, which was specially mounted to celebrate the reopening of the Academy building in 2003; the lower photographs show works by recently elected Academicians and the exhibition **Helen Frankenthaler: Works on Paper** organised by the Royal Scottish Academy.*

▲

The opening exhibition Monet: The Seine and The Sea *occupied most of the upper galleries and attracted over 170,000 visitors during its three month run. The show provided a crucial test of the new facilities in the building such as the goods lift, air-conditioning, security and lighting, all of which performed to the desired standard.*

▲

Sir Timothy Clifford, Director-
General of the National Galleries
of Scotland, Brian Ivory,
Chairman of the Trustees, with
HRH Prince Charles, Duke of
Rothesay at the Monet opening.
Photography by J. Douglas Keegan

Watson Gordon Professor of
Fine Art at the University of
Edinburgh, the curators of the
Monet exhibition, with HRH
Prince Charles, Duke of
Rothesay.
Photography by J. Douglas Keegan

▼

Michael Clarke, Director of the
National Gallery of Scotland and
Director of the Playfair Project,
and Professor Richard Thomson,

▶

View from Hanover Street
showing the Royal Scottish
Academy at the time of the
Monet exhibition in 2003.

With the Academy building successfully reopened attention turned to phase two of the project: the completion and fitting out of the underground link. The original specification included a lecture theatre (200 capacity), education suite, IT gallery, cloak-room, shop, entrance hall and a restaurant (120 capacity). In theory, a visitor would be able to spend a whole day in the complex without having to venture out of doors, as access from the central link to both the National Gallery and the Academy would be provided by elegant circular staircases and lifts. Although the existing entrances to the Gallery and Academy buildings were to be retained, a further grand entrance overlooking East Princes Street Gardens was also planned. Faced with Classach stone, a good match with the stones used for the Gallery and the Academy building, this façade was elegantly styled with rusticated and battered piers that provide a visual base to the whole site when viewed from the east. Such features make fitting reference to the surrounding buildings, in particular the Bank of Scotland which, was substantially remodelled by David Bryce in 1863. It was also punctuated with generously proportioned windows, allowing the maximum amount of light to flood into the underground area of the link. Light was viewed as being of crucial importance in articulating these underground spaces, a lesson learned from the museum schemes of I.M. Pei, in particular the Grand Louvre in Paris. A series of circular roof lights set into the surface of the piazza above were designed by the architect to achieve a mix of natural and artificial light in the space below articulated into neo-Soanian bays. The most spectacular of these windows was placed in a stepped pyramid in the piazza and located directly over the circular information desk in the link concourse. The pyramid itself was slightly rotated, thereby disrupting the strong axial alignment of the existing buildings on the Mound.

In engineering terms, the creation of the structural box containing the underground link proved to be one of the most complex parts of the project. This was achieved by creating a piled wall as close to the existing gallery buildings as possible, propping the walls apart to prevent the weight of the galleries pushing them in, then excavating over 50,000 tons of earth from the Mound to create the required space. The new concrete structure was then built up and included a web of structural columns and a roof slab solid enough to take weights of up to sixty tons, as the precinct still needed to accommodate occasional traffic. Internally, the construction of the new spaces – education rooms, shop, restaurant and visitor facilities – proved more straightforward than had been the case with the Academy refurbishment, although service routes and spaces for mechanical plant had to be shoehorned in very ingeniously. Within East Princes Street Gardens, paths have been adjusted to make access to the entrance easier and to open the views from the Waverley and North Bridges.

▼
Architects' drawing of the completed Playfair Link.

© *John Miller and Partners*

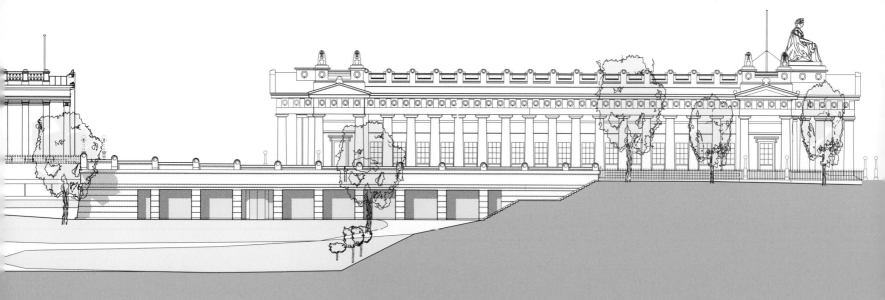

▲

In engineering terms, the creation of the structural box containing the underground link proved to be one of the most complex parts of the project. Over 50,000 tons of earth had to be excavated from the Mound to create the required space.

◄

Although the construction of the new internal spaces in the Link proved more straightforward than had been the case with the Academy refurbishment, ingenious solutions were required to shoehorn in service routes and spaces for mechanical plant.

▶

The concrete structure is heavily reinforced to take full road loadings. The illustration shows some of the thousands of tons of steel rods required for this purpose.

▲

View showing the stepped pyramid under construction in the piazza, which is located directly over the circular information desk in the link concourse below. The pyramid itself, slightly rotated, deliberately disrupts the strong axial alignment of the existing buildings on the Mound.

◀

View of the central concourse showing the IT gallery under construction.

▶

Views from East Princes Street Gardens showing the Playfair Project at an early stage and nearing completion.

Gallery II in the refurbished
Royal Scottish Academy
showing *The Age of Titian*
exhibition (2004). On the end
wall are the two great Titian
paintings, *Diana and Actaeon*
and *Diana and Callisto* on loan
to the National Gallery of
Scotland from the Duke of
Sutherland.

The new East Princes Street Gardens entrance to the Mound complex, shortly after the completion of the Playfair Project in August 2004.

The Farmer Concourse

Previous pages:
the main concourse in the
Weston Link, with the IT
Gallery and Hawthornden
Lecture Theatre beyond.

▲

Behind the information and
ticket sales desk, the Gallery
Shop is seen on the left and
The Gallery Bar and
Restaurant behind the glazed
screen on the right.

◀

The concourse looking east,
daylight floods in from East
Princes Street Gardens.

◄

The Hawthornden Lecture Theatre.

►

The two educational suites, supported by the Gannochy Trust, in the Clore Education Centre.

► (following pages)
The IT Gallery, supported by the Robertson Trust, within the Clore Education Centre.

▲

The Gallery Shop.

▶

The Gallery Bar and Restaurant,
which looks out across East
Princes Street Gardens.

▶

Sir Timothy Clifford, Director-General of the National Galleries of Scotland (left) and Brian Ivory, Chairman of the Trustees of the National Galleries of Scotland (right) escorting HRH Prince Philip and the First Minister, Jack McConnell, to the Weston Link.
Photography by J. Douglas Keegan / Keegan Photography

▶

Brian Ivory and Sir Timothy Clifford with HRH Prince Philip, Duke of Edinburgh after the opening ceremony for the Playfair Project.
Photography by J. Douglas Keegan / Keegan Photography

▶

Michael Clarke, Director of the National Gallery of Scotland and Director of the Playfair Project introducing the architects of the Playfair Project, John Miller and Su Rogers, to HRH Prince Philip, Duke of Edinburgh.
Photography by J. Douglas Keegan / Keegan Photography

▶

Sir Timothy Clifford with HRH Prince Philip, Duke of Edinburgh at the Titian exhibition.
Photography by J. Douglas Keegan / Keegan Photography

▶

From left to right: Brian Ivory, Frank McAveety, Minister for Tourism, Sport, Culture and the Arts, Sir Timothy Clifford, Liz Forgan, Chair of the Heritage Lottery Fund, and Michael Clarke at the gala dinner to celebrate the opening of the Playfair Project and the Titian exhibition.
Photography by J. Douglas Keegan / Keegan Photography

▶

The gala dinner for lenders to the Titian exhibition and the donors to the Playfair Project, which was held in the National Gallery of Scotland.
Photography by J. Douglas Keegan / Keegan Photography

National Galleries of Scotland on The Mound

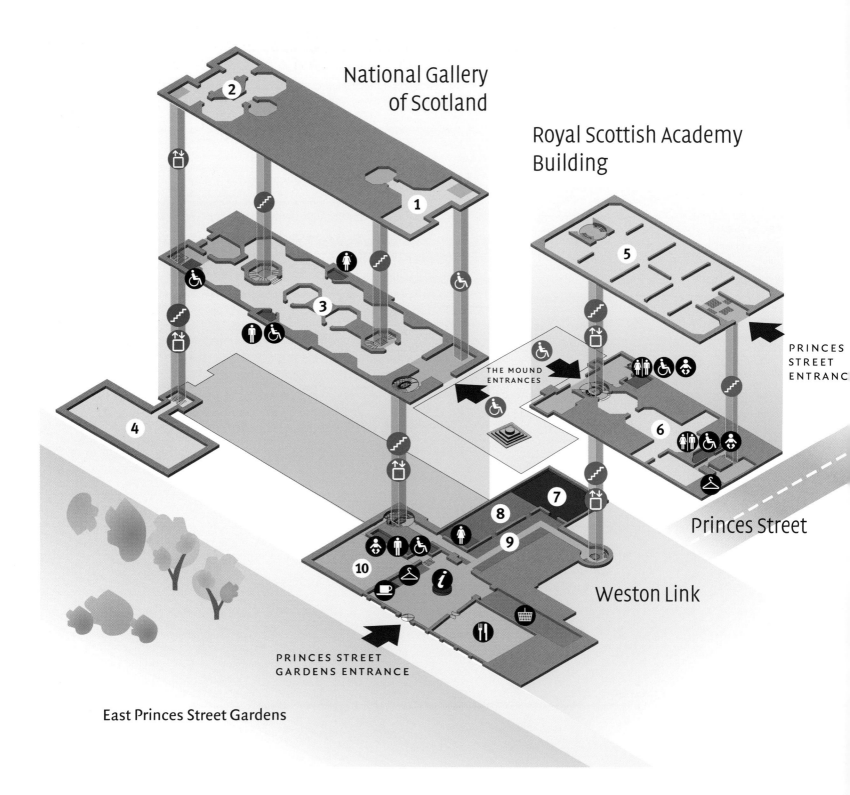

National Gallery of Scotland

Royal Scottish Academy Building

THE MOUND ENTRANCES

PRINCES STREET ENTRANCE

Princes Street

Weston Link

PRINCES STREET GARDENS ENTRANCE

East Princes Street Gardens

NATIONAL GALLERY OF SCOTLAND

1 Upper Galleries: Early Italian & Northern European

2 Upper Galleries: 18th & 19th-Century European, including the French Impressionists

3 Ground Floor: Permanent Collection

4 Lower Galleries: Scottish Collection and Temporary Exhibitions

ROYAL SCOTTISH ACADEMY BUILDING

5 Upper Galleries: Temporary Exhibitions

6 Lower Galleries: Temporary Exhibitions

FACILITIES

 Toilets

 Toilets with Disabled Access

 Baby Change

 Cloakrooms

LINKS

 Entrances

 Stairs

 Lift

 Wheelchair Access

WESTON LINK

7 Hawthornden Lecture Theatre

8 Clore Education Centre

9 IT Gallery

10 Print Room & Research Library

The Gallery Restaurant & Bar

Coffee Bar

Gallery Shop

Information and Exhibition Ticket Sales

CONCLUSION

Major loan exhibitions can now be accommodated in the Academy building following the achievement of phase one of the project in 2003. The construction of the Playfair Project was finished in August 2004 with the completion of phase two. This final phase has allowed the Galleries to provide a full range of much-needed visitor facilities to satisfy the eye, the intellect and the appetite. Of greatest significance are the facilities which enable the Galleries to begin to fulfil their enormous potential in the fields of education and access, opening up their riches to a much wider range of visitors and users, both nationally and internationally. The project has represented a crucial development of the Galleries' estates. It has required a collective act of faith from the Trustees and staff of the National Galleries of Scotland, from the Scottish Executive and all the institutions and individuals who have given such magnificent and generous support. The National Gallery of Scotland and the Royal Scottish Academy, joined at the hip from their respective beginnings, are now well and truly united by virtue of an architectural scheme of which the people of Scotland can feel justifiably proud.

Funders and Donors

AS AT 16 AUGUST 2004

SCOTTISH EXECUTIVE

Heritage Lottery Fund

·EDINBVRGH·
THE CITY OF EDINBURGH COUNCIL

PLAYFAIR FOUNDERS
Bank of Scotland
Ewan and Christine Brown
Richard and Catherine Burns
Cazenove
Clore Duffield Foundation
Dunard Fund
Sir Tom and Lady Farmer
Francis Finlay
The Gannochy Trust
Gavin and Kate Gemmell
Sir Angus and Lady Grossart
Drue Heinz DBE
International Music and Art
    Foundation, Vaduz
Linea d'ombra
Allan and Carol Murray
Stewart and Jannion Newton
PF Charitable Trust
Robertson Trust
The Ross Girls
The Royal Bank of Scotland
Dr Mortimer and Theresa Sackler
    Foundation
The Weston Family
The Wolfson Foundation

PLAYFAIR BENEFACTORS
Binks Trust
The Dulverton Trust
The MacRobert Trust
The Schroder Family
Scottish & Newcastle PLC
Barry and Helen Sealey

PLAYFAIR PATRONS
Robert Barr's Charitable Trust
Mr and Mrs Benjamin Bonas
The Cundill Foundation
Claire Enders
Mr and Mrs James Ferguson
Brian and Oona Ivory
Fred Johnston
Michael and Judith Kennedy
Lloyds TSB Foundation for
    Scotland
The Orrin Chairtable Trust
Mr Derald Ruttenberg
Giles and Ros Weaver

PLAYFAIR DONORS
Aberdeen Asset Management
Irené Archer
The Armet and Murray Families
Lord and Lady Balniel
Barcapel Foundation
Mr and Mrs Graeme Bissett
Sheriff David and Mrs Jean Bogie
Serge and Elizabeth Bouloux
Patrick Bourne
James and Anna Buxton
The Cadogan Charity
Lady Mary Callander
Cruden Foundation
In memory of Arthur Stewart
    Curran
The Evelyn Drysdale Charitable
    Trust
Edinburgh Art Studies
Andrew Fraser
Gordon Fraser Charitable Trust
Simon Gibson Charitable Trust
In memory of Mrs Ruby Gordon
Mr and Mrs Raymond Green
Mrs J. Donald Hardie
Havelock Europa PLC
The Hedley Foundation
The Hope Scott Trust
Mr and Mrs Dermot Jenkinson
Mrs E.A. Johnston

Tom and Joan Johnston
Mr and Mrs Peter Kimmelman
The Kinpurnie Column
The Landale Charitable Trust
The Leckie Column
A.G. Leventis Foundation
Ronald and Rita McAulay
Harvey McGregor
The Mainhouse Charitable Trust
Mr and Mrs James Manclark
Martin Currie Investment
    Management Ltd
The Mayshiel Estate
John Menzies plc
Mrs Jean Miller
The Morrison Foundation
Mr and Mrs G. Malcolm Murray
In memory of Jean and Bussy
    Nimmo
D.F.J. Paterson
Sir William Purves
The Rank Foundation
Sir Alick and Lady Rankin
Scotbelge Charitable Trust
In memory of Robert, Meta and
    Alec Stevenson
Peter Stormonth Darling
    Charitable Trust
W. Syson in memory of Beatrice
    Huntington
Britt Tidelius
The Trusthouse Charitable
    Foundation
Turcan Connell WS
Mrs Archibald Walker
In memory of Dr Isobel A. White
The Zachs-Adam Family

Mrs Dawn Abbott
Adam and Company plc
Mrs Elizabeth Adam
Mrs Margaret Adam
Dr A.D. Adams
Christine Adams
Mr L. Adams
Mrs R. Adams
Fiona Adamson
The ADAPT Trust
M. and P. Ahrens
Mrs M. Ainsworth
Lady Airey
The Countess of Airlie
Catherine Aitken
To the 'Jacks of all Trades' J.A.
Lena Robb by Dr R. MacG. Aitken
T. Aitken
Mrs Alderson
Mrs J.K. Aldred and Mrs Jane
    Moore
Dr Isobel Alexander
Joyce Alexander
James Allan
Stuart Allan
Dr V.J.M. Allen
Mr K.F. Allbeson
Mr P. Allinson
Marie Allison
Doug Allsop
H. Anderson
V. Anderson
Dr John L. Anderton
Mrs Dorothea R. Andrews
Louise Annand
In memory of William and Mary
    Armour
Joanne Armstrong
Elizabeth Armstrong-Wilson
Carolina Arnold
Robin Arnott
C.S.G. Arthur
Eileen M. Atkinson
Ms Valerie Atkinson
'J.J. Audubon exhibited here 1826'
G.G. Auld
Ms Katherine Awramenko
The Ayrshire Decorative and Fine
    Arts Society
Mr G.M. Bagot
A.K. Bain
Mr John Baines
Baldoukie Trust
The Tekoa Trust
Geoff and Mary Ball
Mrs A. Ballantyne
Patricia Barclay
Mrs Susan Barnes
Virginia Barnes
J.P. Barnet
Mr and Mrs Oliver Barratt
Remembering Mardi Barrie, artist
Mardi Barrie
E. Barrowman
Paul and Sharron Bassett
Mr and Mrs John Batty
Gordon and Ena Baxter
    Foundation
Mary R. Baxter
Mr Robert Bayliss
Angels Beardsley
Mrs R. Beattie

Lady Beaumont
Mr C.A. Beckett
Peter Beckett
Miss Helen Bee
M. Beeston
Bridget Begbie
Mr Andrew Bell
Dorothy Winifred Bell
Ms Elaine Bell
Mrs M. Bell
Margo Bell
Martin Bell
Nancy Bell
Mrs Patricia Bell
Mr B.A. Bembridge
N. Benigan
Shirley and Peter Bennett
Mr and Mrs F.V. Bennetts
Elizabeth Beran
William and Elizabeth Berry
The Hon. Mrs Best
Andrew Betchley
Deirdre Bett
L.M. Betteridge
Mrs Eleanor Bevan
Ailsa Bhattacharya
Mrs Grace Blackhall
Mrs M. Blake
Sir Michael and Lady Blake
Mrs Rosemary Bland
Mrs Mary A. Blood
Tony and Katrina Blythe
Mr and Mrs William Boggon
Mrs Alice Bold
Miss Anthea Bond
Ms Anne Bonnar
Mrs N.A. Bonner
Mrs P. Boon
Dr Eve Borland
Philip Borrowman
Dr Richard A. Bowie
Mr William Bowie
Sir Alan and Lady Bowness
Mrs Alma Boyack
Moreen and Gordon Boyd
Mr O.A. Boyle and Ms L. Bell
Ms Kath Bradley
E. Brand
Ms Barbara Braneu
Mr and Mrs Peter Branscombe
Michael and Barbara Breaks
Judith Brearley
Ann Bredin
Mr and Mrs Francis Brewis
For Elizabeth and Tom Briggs
Constance Brodie
Dr Patrick W. Brooks
Elizabeth R. Brown
Mr and Mrs J. Brown
Margaret Brown
Thomas and Ellinder Brown
Mrs Isobel Brownrigg
Mr Iain Bruce
Margaret Bryson
Janey Buchan
Nigel Buchanan
Catherine I. Buick
L.M. Burley
Mr A.D. Burnett
Mr and Mrs Joe Burnett-Stuart
In loving memory of David
    Burnside

Ms Burton
Mr K.M. Bury
John Busby
Thomas F. Bush
Mr Douglas Butler
Vincent Butler
Mr P.G. Buttars
Sir David and Lady Butter
The Byrom Family
Alistair Cairns and Robin Rice
Mr Kenneth F. Cairns
Mrs Margaret Calder
Lord Cameron of Lochbroom
A.M. Cameron
E.M. Cameron
The Rt Hon. the Lord Provost
    Elizabeth Cameron
George Cameron
Helen L. Cameron
Izzy Cameron
Mrs K. Cameron and
    Ms O. Fulinova
Mrs M.E. Cameron
Dr R.C.P. Cameron
Mrs A.M. Campbell
Mr D.A. Campbell
Ms Fiona Campbell
Mr and Mrs I.M. Campbell
J. Campbell
Julia Campbell
Mrs K.C. Campbell
M. Campbell
Mr Toby Campbell
Iris and Robert Cansdale
M. Carr
Mr John Carson
Mr J. Cassels
Ms Beth Cavanagh
Mrs Ann Challoner
Mr Alan M.M. Chalmers
Mr Hugh Chalmers
Sheila Chamberlin
Ann Chandley
Joan E. Chapman
Mrs E.V. Charity
Mrs Elizabeth Chatswin
Mr William Cherrie
John Chiene
Mrs Shelia Christie
Christie's
Colin E. Christison
Mr Richard Church-Michael
In memory of Eugene Cines,
    New York
G. Clapperton
Mrs Dorothy Clark
Elizabeth Clark
Jane Clark
Linda Clark
Dr R.M. Clark
R. Clark
Michael and Deborah Clarke
Jean Clarkson
Mrs Georgina Clayton
George Cleland
Mr and Mrs G. Clemson
Elizabeth, Lady Clerk
Sir Timothy and Lady Clifford
Brenda Clouston, sculptor
Katrina Clow
Lady Clyde
Clydesdale Bank plc

June and Michael Cochrane
Mrs N.P. Cockerill
June Cocksedge
Mr and Mrs Ernest Coghill
The Vivienne and Sam Cohen
    Charitable Trust
Dr D.F. Collecott
Professor Collee, with my
    admiration
Frank Collieson
Mrs M. Collins
Beryl Colquhoun
Mrs I. Coltart
Sheila Colvin and Nicholas
    Phillipson
Dr David Colvin
Compton and Mouse
Mr Charles Connell
Mrs Tugela Connell
Elizabeth Conran
Tom and Jan Conway
Mr C.L. Cook
David Coombs
In memory of Lindsay L. Cooper
Susan Cormack
Joyce Cottle
Anne Couch, Teacher of Art and
    Design
Miss E. Ann Couper
E.W. Coutts
Brigadier Colin Hunter Cowan
Mr and Mrs I.R. Cowan
Mrs Joyce Cowan
In memory of Sir Robert Cowan
W.M. Cowan
Mrs V. Coward
E.S. Cowell
Janet Cowlishaw
Mr Marc Cox
P.A. Cox
Mrs E. Craig
Jean Craig
William A. Craig
Mrs Helen Craik
Mr Derek J. Cran
Mrs Marguerite Crane
Mrs Dorothea Crawford
Lyle Crawford C.A.
Mrs D.E. Crichton
Mrs J. Patricia Crichton
Dr T.I. Crichton
Mr Ronald Crighton
P. Croall
P.A. and T.K. Crombie
Mr Brian M. Crook
Mrs P. Crosfield
Kitty Cruft
A.J. Cruikshank
R. John Cruse
Deborah Cumming
Mrs Julia Cumming
Kevin T. Cummings
J. Cuninghame
Captain and Mrs Ronald
    Cunningham-Jardine
Dr I.D. and Mrs E.M. Currie
The Earl of Dalkeith
Mrs M. Dallas
Dr Malcolm Dando
Avril Darby
N. Davey
Mr John Davidson

Elizabeth Ann Davies
Miss Janet Davies
Mrs Mary Yates Davis
James Dawnay
Lady Jane Dawnay
Anne and Ray Dean
Dr Sheila Dean
Mrs C.A. Denison-Pender
Mrs G.A.J. Dennison
Mrs Elizabeth Dent
Dr J.S. Dent
In memory of Beryl Derbyshire
Andrew Dewar-Durie CBE
Mrs Elspeth Dewhurst
J. Dickinson
James Dickson-Leach
Mr John R. Dilks
Ian and Mary Dobinson
Francis, Alison, Charlotte and
    Katy Docherty
Mrs Ann V. Dockrell
Raymond and Doreen Dodd
Miss Margaret Dodds
Andrew and Anne Doig
J.M. Donaghy
Miss Anne Donald
Mrs Donalda J. Donald
Alan Donaldson
Professor Margaret Donaldson
Mandy Donoghue
Mrs T. Dorati
Ms Shona Dougall
Loudon Downs
Roberta Doyle
Mr and Mrs D.A. Drake
Fiona Drinnan
Leslie Allan Drummond (artist)
Garnett Charitable Trust
Mr Stanley H. Duffus
Mrs M. Duffy
Dum Spiro Spero
Sir James Dunbar-Nasmith
Miss Anne Duncan
The Countess of Dundee
Mr and Mrs Ian Dunlop
For Johnnie Dunmore who had a
    love for the finer things of
    life
Hazel Dunn
Dunphail Charitable Trust
Frank and Lorna Dunphy
Katie Durkin
K. Duval and C. Hamilton
Mr and Mrs Maurizio Dwek
Chris and Jane Eadie
Dorothy Ann Eadie
Miss Elizabeth East
In memory of George, Christina,
    Florence and Dorothy Ebbs
James Edgar
Mr and Mrs R.E. Edgar
Edinburgh Antiques and Fine Arts
    Society
Edinburgh Old Town Association
Lady Edmonstone
Mr Robert Edwards
Mrs J.P. Elliot
M.L. Elgin
Elizabeth 21.9.1958–17.4.1996
Marc Ellington
Alan Elliot
G.B. Elliot

Mr and Mrs R.J. Elliot
Dr Rose Elliott
Mr and Mrs C.C.G. Ellis
Mr A.A. Elsdon
Emma and Hannah and Tessa
The Endrick Trust
Mr and Mrs D.J. Essery
Mrs E. Eunson
Sally and Nick Evans
Carl Evans
Mrs Jane Eyre
John and Shelia Fairbairn
S. Farmer
John and Isobel Fearn
Mrs Kathryn S. Fegan
Susan and Mitchell Feinberg
Alison Ferguson – in memory of
    my husband Tommy
Miss Joan P.S. Ferguson
Hector Fernandez
Mrs Hilary Ferrand
Sebastian de Ferranti
Elizabeth Ferrard
Mrs Aileen Ferrigan
Mrs F. Fielding
Emilie Filmer-Wilson
Mrs Anne Finlayson
Niall and Dale Finlayson 2004
Martin Firth and Mary Rose
Mr P.R. Fisk
Linda Fitzpatrick
Mrs Cherry Fleming
Mr Ian J. and Mrs
    Margaret F.K. Fleming
John E.E. Fleming
Hilary Flenley
Andrew Fletcher
Mrs P.D. Flood
Helen J. Forbes
Mr G.A. Ford
L.M. Ford
Peter Ford
Alex Forsyth
Dr W. Fortescue
Hon. John Dewar Charitable Trust
Lord and Lady Forteviot
Lorna Foster
Mrs Jean E. Fowlie
Fiona Douglas-Home
Mairi Fraser
M.K. Fraser
Ellen Freeman
Iain and Rosemary Freeman
T.G. Freshwater
In loving memory of Tom Gallie
Mrs D. Gardiner
Ms Alexandra Gardner
Miss R.S. Garrett
Alison Geissler
Robert Gemmell
P. Gerard
Mrs Deanna Gerber
Alistair Gibb
Glen Gibb
Mrs Jennifer Gibb
Mrs Lavinia Gibbs
Dr Angus Gibson
Ellen and Archie Gibson
Margaret and John Gilchrist
Cecily and Margaret Giles
Ms Margaret Gilfillan
Charles Gimingham
Geraldine Girvan

Dr E. Glen
Mr and Mrs J.R. Glen
Mr and Mrs Glendinning
Miss Daphne Godson
Mr and Mrs Douglas Goodall
Sir Matthew Goodwin's Charitable
    Trust
C. Ralph Gordon
Mr and Mrs Ian Gordon
Mrs Judith Gordon
Mr W.P. Gordon
Robert Goudy
Mr Paul Grace
The Graham Family
Mrs Patricia Graham
Mr R.M. Graham
Mrs Graham-Marr
E. Graham-Yooll
Mr and Mrs Grant
Lady Grant
Mr and Mrs Keith Grant
Rev Canon A. Grant
Miss Yvonne R.F. Grant
Mr and Mrs John Grant-Wood
Ms Ellen Graves
Andrew and
    Elizabeth Gray
J.A. Gray
Mrs Joanna Gray
Ms Wendy Gray
Miss S. Green
Mrs W.O. Greenaway
D. Greengrass
Mrs M.E. Grier
Dr A. Grieve
Ivor Guild
Marion Dunn
Kim Gunningham
Mrs I.A. Guthrie
Mrs Mary Haggart O B E
Elspeth Hall
Mr and Mrs Ian Hall
Miss Isobel Hall
Mr and Mrs Halliday
Elizabeth Halliday
Dr and Mrs John Halliday
Dr E.F. Hamilton
Mr John A. Hamilton
Nancy Hammond
Ruth Hannah
James Harrigan
The Reverend and Mrs W.F. Harris
Mrs E.M. Harrison
Iain and Fabienne Harrison
Susan Harrison
Mr R. Harrower
Dr Janina M. Harvey
Mrs A. Harvey-Jamieson
Eileen Havard-Williams
Michael Havinden
Mrs A. Hawley-Groat
Mr and Mrs Alexander Hay
Mr A.W. Hay
Miss J.E. Hay
Mr D. Henderson
Ms Kathleen Henderson
Miss Kathryn Henderson
Ruth Henderson
David and Joan Henry
Miss J. Herkes
Mr Gary E. Heron
Ms S. Hewitt
Mrs Moira E. Heywood

Jean Higginson
Mrs Joanna Highton
Sean Hignett
In memory of Nigel J.W. Hill L L B,
    from his family
Mrs Paulette M. Hill
Mr and Mrs James Hill
The Terpsichore Trust
Maureen Hobbs
Mrs G. Hodgson
M.C. Hogarth
Miss M.D. Hogarth M B E
Mrs M.E. Hogg
Mr Peter Hoggan
Mrs C.G. Holden
Stephen Holland
Mrs N.R. Holmyard
Janette Holt
Mr and Mrs W. Holt
Lord Hope of Craighead
Emily Hope
Kozo Hoshino
Melanie Houldsworth
Mrs P. Housley
Moira Houston
Drs Peter and Janet Howell
Mrs E.N. Howitt
Hugh and Mo
Mrs P. Hughes
Dr and Mrs D. Hughson
Robert Hume
Ms Alison Hunter
Miss L. Hunter
James Hunter-Blair
Fatima Irene Huq
Mr C.G.I. and Mrs A.B.M. Hussell
Mrs Sue Hussin
Mr and Mrs P. Hutton
Mr and Mrs Michael Iles
Inches Carr Trust
Mrs E. Inglis
James Innes
Mr and Mrs M.W. Innes
Mrs C.R. Irvine
D.H. Irvine
Mrs Sylvia J. Irvine
Ms Sheena Irving
Mr and Mrs W.R. Irving
Mrs S. Jackson
Mr and Mrs Keith James
Mrs L.G. James
Mr and Mrs J.P. Jameson
Mr and Mrs David Jamieson
Gemma Jamieson
Mr Edward W. Jarah
John Jarvis-Smith and Roger Cave
Mr and Mrs Gordon Jefferson
Mrs Nora Jenkinson
I. Adele Jennison
P.L. Johnson
Dr and Mrs J. Johnston
Mrs J.M. Johnston
Margaret A.L. Johnston
Mary Johnston
Miss Maureen Johnston
Mr Maxwell Johnston
Miss Rosemary Johnston
Sir Raymond and Lady Johnstone
Professor and Mrs Charles Jones
Ms Felicity Jones
Grace Jordan
Robyn Ross Jordan
Ms Jeanette Joseph

Miss Yuka Kadoi
Mrs Catherine Kay
Mrs June Kean
Mrs Irene Keating
Mr Roy Keil
Miss Jane Kellett
Kirsteen Kelly
R. Kelly
Prof. and Mrs C.J.H. Kelnar
Mrs E. Kennedy
Gavin and Patricia Kennedy
Mrs D.M. Kent
Sir John and Lady Anne Kerr
Miss M. Kerr
Ralph Bruce Kerr
Dr Susan Kerr
Mr William Kerr
Michael Graham Kidd
Mr Adam King
Mr Graeme King
John King
Lady Kinnaird
Mr Thomas Kinsey
A.W. Kirkland
J. Kirkpatrick
J.C. Kitchin
Mrs Rupert de Klee
Dr Gabriel Kuhn
Dr P.M. Kumar
Mrs B. Kyle
Georgina Kynaston
Madeleine and Kitty Lagneau
Lord Laing of Dunphail Charitable
    Trust
Barbara Laing
Mr and Mrs Gordon Laird
Dr Helen Laird
Miss Sandra Lamb
Hilary Lane
Mrs Irene Lang
Mr Eric Larsen
Mr Damon de Laszlo
Mr J.G. Latham
Douglas Law
Mrs M. Law
Mr M. Leates
Ms Marie Leckie
Mrs Bruce Leeming
Jessie Leggat
In memory of the late Steven Leith
The Lendrum Charitable Trust
Mrs Kirsty Leonard
Mrs Elizabeth Leslie
Norman and Christine Lessels
Mr and Mrs P.J. Lewis
Jeremy Lewison
Mrs J.M. Lindesay-Bethone
Mr P. Lindow
Laura Lindsay
G. and O. Lindsay
Alison Linklater-Betley
Dr Doris Livingstone
Mrs R. Lochhead
For Russell Lockhart
Christina Lodder
Ms M.E.C. Loggie
Mrs Alison Loraine
Mr and Mrs G. Lord
Ms Jenny Lorimer
Mr Ian Lornie
Joan Loudon
I.F. Lowe
Sir Ian and Lady Lowson

Dr and Mrs C.P. Lowther
Mrs Lukas
Mrs E. Lutz
Mr and Mrs A. Lyburn
A. Lynch
Lytham St Annes U 3 A Art
    Appreciation Group
Dr and Dr G.M. McAndrew
Ms W.M. Macaulay
Mr and Mrs Hugh Macdiarmid
Mr and Mrs D.J. Macdonald
Mr and Mrs Iain Macdonald
Mrs Jeanette MacDonald
In memory of Helen and John
    Henry Macdonell
Lord and Lady Macfarlane of
    Bearsden
June Macfarlane Cohen
Kirsty Macgregor
G.C. Mackintosh
Mr and Mrs D. Gordon Macintyre
Mrs L.M. MacIver
Mrs Marion Macivor
Angus and Elizabeth Mackay
J. Mackay
Lady Lucinda Mackay
Miss Shelia Mackay
Mrs M. MacKenzie
Arthur Christopher Mackenzie
Barbara MacKenzie
Miss Diana Mackenzie
Mrs Emma Mackenzie
Mrs M.J.D. Mackenzie
Ms Rhoda Mackenzie
Mr and Mrs Philip Mackenzie Ross
Miss Sheila Mary MacKenzie
Gordon Mackie
Katherine Mackie
Mr and Mrs Jim Mackintosh
Dr F.B. Maclaren
Hamish and Fionna Macleod
Mrs J. MacLeod
June Macleod
Frances Macmillan
Jean Macnab
Lt. Col. W.P.C. MacNair
Mr Charles MacQueen
The Mactaggart Third Fund
W.F. MacTaggart
Mrs E.M. McBride
Jean McBurnie
Ms M.T. McCafferty
Professor Alexander McCall Smith
Mr and Mrs David McCallum
Dr Margaret McCance
Ms Anne McCarthy
Mrs C.S. McLean
Brenda McConkey
The McCorquodale Charitable
    Trust
Catherine E. McCracken and Mrs
    Helen E. Wightman
Mr J.M. McDiarmid
Mr A. McDonald
Evelyn McDonald
G.M. McDonald
Mr Douglas McDougall
Mrs I. McDougall – for beauty lives
    with kindness
Mrs K.C. McEachran
Zoe Patricia McFadzean
Mrs V.M. McFarland
Caroline J. McFarlane

S. E. McGilchrist
Patricia McHale, Derbyshire
Kirsty McHugh
Mr A.A.C. McInnes
Mr Finlay McIntosh
Mrs Karina McIntosh
Sally McIntosh
Donald B. McIntyre
Robert McIntyre
Mrs Anne McIver
I. McKee
Douglas and Louisa McKenzie
Matthew Steel McKerrow
Mrs M. McKerrow
Mr Duncan McKichan
Mr G.W. McLachlan
Anita McLaren
Ian McLeod, Nantwich, Cheshire
John McLeod
Violet S. McLeod, Aberdeen
Ms Paquita McMichael
K.I.C. McMillan
Mrs J. A. McNaughton
Mrs Mathilda McNeill
Graham and Elizabeth McNicol
Jolee McPhail
Albert McPhee
Liz McPhillips
Mr and Mrs R. McQuillin
Ms Margaret McSorley
Mrs Mary Main
Jacek and Ursula Makowski
Blair Malcolm
Mr J.V.G. Mallet
The Countess of Mansfield and
    Mansfield
Raye Marcus
Maureen Marnie
Moira Marrian
Campbell Mars
Muriel Mars
Lawrence and Morag Marshall
Mr David Martin
Mrs Doreen M. Martin
J. Martin
Mrs Marjory Martin
Fiona Martynoga
Ian and Elizabeth Mason
Lucy Mason
Nancie Massey Charitable Trust
Mr Gordon C. Massie
Barbara Mathie
Mr Mathieson
Ailish Isabelle Matthee
Mr and Mrs R.H. Maudslay
Mrs M.S. Maudsley
Diana Maxtone Graham
Aileen May, Kirriemuir, Scotland
Ranald and Jennifer Shewan May
Mr J.A.C. Meek
John Meikle
Dr Maureen Meikle
Mr and Mrs William Meikle
Mr and Mrs C. Melville
Dr and Mrs W.D. Melvin
Sir James and Lady Menter
Mrs A.R. Menzies
Norah Menzies 1909–2003
Mrs A. Messenger
Ann Messer
David Michie
In memory of John Midgley
Heather Millar

Mrs Janet Millar
Mrs A. Millar-Craig
Mrs Anne Miller
Ms A.G. Miller
Mr Innes Miller
James and Iris Miller
Margaret Miller
Sir Ronald and Lady Miller
Mrs Rosemary Miller
Ms G.B. Mills
Dr Raymond Mills
Mrs Marie-Anne Milne
Priscilla Minay
The Mitchell Trust
Mrs Nan Mitchell
Mrs W. Mitchell
Mrs Fiona Mitchell-Rose
Mrs Margaret Moffat
Mrs Dagné Moggie
Mrs Ann Moir
Mrs Eunice Mole
Mrs J.G. Molineux
Mrs J.P. Montgomery
Mrs Margaret Moodie
Mrs Sheila Moohan
Brenda E. Moon
John Moore
R.S. Moore
The Earl of Moray
Mr George Morfee
Mr and Mrs B. Morgan
Mrs Lindsay Morison
Mrs Hazel Morrison
James and Dorothy Morrison
Beatrice Morton
Margaret Morton
Miss J.B. Moss
Mrs Patricia Moxey
Dr and Mrs A.R. Muir
Miss Hannah Mulder
Christine Munro
Mr Douglas Munro
Mrs Arthur Munro Ferguson
Rosemary Munro
Murray Art Group, East Kilbride
Mrs G. Murray
Mr J. Murray
J. Murray
John Y. Murray
Kathleen Murray
Norma Y. Murray
Mr and Mrs J.H. Mutch
David and Vivienne Muxworthy
Rosheen Napier
Mr Andrew Neil
S.E. Neill
Alex and Patricia Neish
The Neish Trust
Ella and Andy Neustein
D.K. Newbigging Foundation
Ms R.A. Newton
The Nicoll Family
In memory of Jean and Bussy
    Nimmo
Mr and Mrs Noble
Dr Henry Noltie
Mr Douglas Norrie
Mrs Olive Norrie
Mr Brendan O'Connor
Mrs R. Oddy
M. O'Gorman
Peter Oldfield
Mrs Valerie Oldham

Mrs Patricia O'Neill
The Meyer Oppenheim Trust
Mr Sandy Orr
Michael Orr Paterson
Mr Donald Oswald
Mrs Doris Otto
Mrs Helen Outram
Linda Owens
Mrs Shelia Page
A.F. Park
Tanya Parker
Mrs Christine Parkinson
Mr James Parr
Mrs A. Parry
Mrs Alison Paterson
M.M. Paterson
R.H. Paterson
Mr and Mrs Tom Paterson
Margaret Paton
Mr and Mrs Bruce Patrick
A.I. Patterson
Mr and Mrs Mark Pattinson
Mr and Mrs D.G. Pattle
Maureen S. Pattullo
Michael and Christina Paulson-
    Ellis
Mr F.S.G. Pearson
Mr and Mrs Michael Pearson
Mr and Mrs Stephen Pearson
Mrs E.M. Peattie
Margaret Peden
Jim and Victoria Peers
Mrs E.M.F. Pentland
Dr Sheena Petrie
Mrs Helena Pettie
Miss Shona Pettigrew
John S. Pickles
John and Elizabeth Picton
Mrs Ruth A. Pierce
Mrs Helen Pitkethly
Jeff Pitt
Jean Playfair
Mrs Lucy Poett
Sheena Pollock
Sheriff I.A. Poole
Henry Potts
J. Lowri Potts
Mr Roger Pountain and
    Ms A. Foster
Mrs Marnel Powell
Mr and Mrs W. Pratt
Dr Majory Primrose
Andrew and Joyce Pringle
Lord and Lady Prosser
Alan and Irene Pugh
Mrs M.J. Pullan
Mrs J. Punton
Frank Quigley
Mr and Mrs D.D. Quinn
Brenda Rack
Mr Stephen Rae
Miss N. Rait and Ms F.M.H. Rait
Mrs Nora Ramage
Barbara Ramsey
Major General Charles A. Ramsay
    CB OBE
Mr and Mrs James Ramsay
Mrs Priscilla Ramsey
Patricia Randall
Mrs Margaret Randall
Mrs G. Rankin
Mrs Mary H.F. Rankin
Mrs S.L. Rankin

Mrs Anne E. Rankine
Ms Qatrinnada Rawi
Frank and Sybil Reeder
Philip Reeves
Mr A.D.B. Reid
Mr A.L. Reid
A.W. Reid
Mr and Mrs David Reid
Miss Elizabeth S. Reid
Mrs Marjorie Reid
Anne Reilly
Tom Reilly
Mr Lessel J.C. Rennie
David Rewcastle
Mrs Helma Reynolds
Lady Richardson
Mrs Isabel Richardson
J.A. Riddell
Mr and Mrs Andrew Riddick
Mrs C.M. Riddle
Miss S. Riddle
Sir Malcolm Rifkind
The Risk Charitable Fund
A. Ritch
Andrew Ritchie
Mrs Elizabeth Rivers-Bulkeley
Michael Rix
G.D. Robb
Mrs Catherine A. Robbie
Dr Elizabeth Roberts
Dr Adam A. Robertson
Ms Ann Robertson
Mrs Anna Robertson
Mr and Mrs D.B. Robertson
Mr D.J. Robertson
In memory of Giles H. Robertson
Mrs H. Robertson
Mary K. Robertson
Adam Robson
Godfrey Robson
Ms Dorothy Rodger
Deborah Rolland
Mrs Jeanette Rolland
Mrs Jennifer Romero
Mr Hugh Rorrison
Mr John Rose
Dr Nigel Rose
The Countess of Rosebery
C. Ross
Dr Helen Ross
Mrs Hilary Ross
Mr Magnus Ross
In memory of Carmine Rossi
Royal Academy of Arts
Mrs R. Royles
Mr and Mrs E.J. Rozendaal
Mrs Robyn Ruane
P.A. Ruddle
In memory of Sir Stephen
    Runciman
Mr Ian Rushbrook
Irene Russell
Mrs Tristan Russell
Mrs Joan Rustrick
In loving memory David Jackson
    Rutherford
Dorothy Ryle
Mr and Mrs A.R. Sabine
R. Sacks
Mr and Mrs David Salmon
Heather Salzen neé Fairlie
Mrs E. Samson
Mrs S.A. Sandow

Jackie Sansbury
Adrian Sassoon
Mr Ross Saunders
Deborah Saxton
Mrs R.G. Schaw-Miller
Sheriff and Mrs G. Shiach
Professor Schweizer
Ms Irene A. Scobie
In memory of Kathleen Scogings
Mrs A. Scott
Anne M. Scott
Mrs G. Victoria M. Scott
Mrs Jennifer Scott
Dr Richard and Mrs Rita Scott
Miss S. Scott
Mr W. Scott
Mrs D.M. Scott-Duncan
Mrs A.P. Scott-Moncrieff
Mr and Mrs S.M. Seaman
Mr and Mrs James Seaton
Mrs V. Seery
Nigel and Patricia Seligman
Selkirk Charitable Trust
J.P. Sellars
Mr and Mrs Semple
J.L. Semple
Mr and Mrs R. Seton-Browne
Mr and Mrs James Shanks
Katherine Sharpe
Gilbert Shaw-Dunn
Miss Fiona Shepherd
Frances Shepherd
Ms Heloise Shewan
Mr and Mrs J. Sibbet
Miss H.J. Sidwell
Dr Ann Silver
Mrs Margaret Silver
Christine Sim
Connie Simmers
Ralph Simmonds
Richard Simon
Olive Simpson
Mr Cecil Sinclair
Helen and Neil Sinclair
K. Sinclair
Dr W. Sircus
Dr Norman Skillen
Mr J.G. Skinner
Mr Thomas Skinner
Margaret L. Slater
Mrs A. Sloan
Jean Sloan
Alastair and Carola Small
Miss C.A.M. Smart
Brendan Smith
D. Smith and J. Pond
J.C. Smith
M.G.H. Smith
Mrs Margaret T. Smith
Mrs Patricia Smith
The Hon. Philip Smith
R.M. Smith
Mr W.N. Smith
Ms Pernille Smout
Ms Harriet Smyth
David and Moyra Smythe
Horace I. Snaith
Mrs M.S. Snowdon
D.A. Spencer
Mrs K.B. Spurgin
Mrs J.C. Stanton
Miss Caroline Staples
Mr R.J. Starling

Published by the Trustees of the National Galleries of
Scotland on the occasion of the completion of the Playfair
Project in August 2004

© The Trustees of the National Galleries of Scotland
ISBN 1 903278 59 7

Designed and typeset in Quadraat by Dalrymple
Colour repro by Transcolour, Edinburgh
Printed and bound in Poland by OZGraf S.A.

Front cover: View of the Playfair Project with Edinburgh
Castle in the background

Frontispiece: Model of the Playfair Project

SELECT BIBLIOGRAPHY
C. Thompson, Pictures for Scotland, Edinburgh, 1972
I. Gow and T. Clifford, The National Gallery of Scotland:
An Architectural and Decorative History, Edinburgh, 1998

AUTHOR'S ACKNOWLEDGEMENTS
I am most grateful to my colleagues Janis Adams,
Christopher Baker, Timothy Clifford, Valerie Hunter, Scott
Robertson, Sheila Scott, and Christine Thompson for their
assistance during the writing of this publication, which has
been expertly designed by Robert Dalrymple. Michael Clarke

PHOTOGRAPHIC CREDITS
All interior and exterior shots by Keith Hunter Photography
unless otherwise stated.
© Keith Hunter and the National Galleries of Scotland 2004